GETTING RICH

How To Avoid
Being RIPPED-OFF
By The Insurance Industry

From The International Best Selling Authors

Dr. Denis Cauvier & Alan Lysaght

ISBN 978-0-9733549-7-3

First Edition, First Printing – Copyright © 2016 by Wealth Solutions Press

Second edition July 2016

Edited by Judi Blaze

Cover design and layout by Syed Muhammad Salman

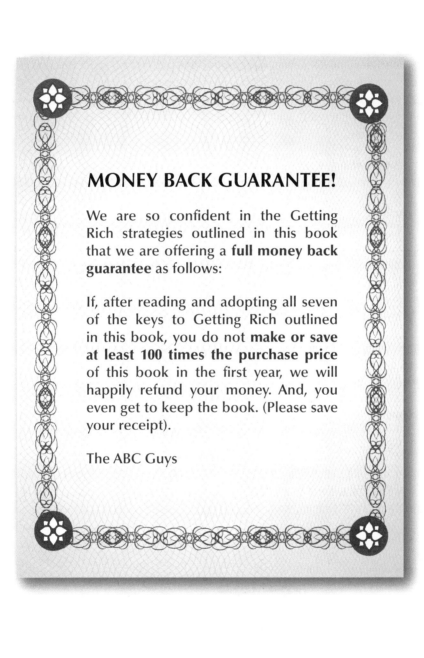

MONEY BACK GUARANTEE!

We are so confident in the Getting Rich strategies outlined in this book that we are offering a **full money back guarantee** as follows:

If, after reading and adopting all seven of the keys to Getting Rich outlined in this book, you do not **make or save at least 100 times the purchase price** of this book in the first year, we will happily refund your money. And, you even get to keep the book. (Please save your receipt).

The ABC Guys

Contents

Getting Rich

Introduction

> " Americans collectively lose about **$17 Billion a year to conflicted retirement account advice.**
>
> Senator Elizabeth Warren[1] "

It is a sad reality that so many people have bought into the myth that average and ordinary folks can't get rich. They believe that it's something mysterious that happens to others who are more highly educated or more sophisticated people than themselves. It's not true! We've met thousands of people who went from being in a seemingly hopeless financial position to what most people would call rich. All they did was to make some fundamental yet simple changes that, literally, altered the course of their lives. Once you understand the seven keys of getting rich covered in this book you can create the life of your dreams.

In this book we will outline many simple strategies that can save you significant amounts of money and, when invested wisely, over time will grow into huge savings for you and your family's future. One of the key areas of savings we're looking at in this book is the type of life insurance people buy. This one item alone could be robbing you of hundreds of dollars *every month*. Think about what that could mean to you over the course of 30+ years. Millions of people hold policies like these that they don't really understand, while millions more have a real need for the protection of insurance, but don't have any.

(1) October, 2015 report.

For the past 15 years we made our position very clear in our books and workshops. Specifically, we believe that the vast majority of North Americans should "**buy inexpensive Term life insurance and do something intelligent with the money you save.**" Recently we've examined a tremendous number of policies held by average people. Our findings were shocking. Unbeknownst to these innocent people, they had been paying tens of thousands of dollars – and in several cases, hundreds of thousands of dollars – and ended up with virtually no savings at all. And, no, these weren't policies from companies operating out of seedy back alleys; these were from Fortune 500 companies. One of the executives of the companies involved, who was on the fast track to the C Suite, called it a "racket" before quitting the industry. Read the stories we've collected; you will be amazed. We were. Examining just this one small piece of your financial picture could instantly change the direction of your path to financial freedom.

The fact is that you don't need a fancy degree, a massive income, or the winning lottery numbers to build wealth. All you have to do is read this book cover to cover, apply the strategies offered, and your finances will quickly turn around.

If it's so simple, why then doesn't everybody do it? Well, why doesn't everybody go to the gym? It's the same kind of question. We know we should be doing it, but we're too intimidated to take the first step. Once we do, things change. People get passionate about their physical health or their financial health. And they end up feeling much better about themselves as a result.

When we were working with our creative design team on the cover, we looked at several hundred photos to find the single picture that would capture the essence of this book. The image we chose is very powerful because it represents two simultaneous actions: money going down a drain or money growing and piling up towards wealth. The point is, people who read this book and use all of the seven keys it describes will get richer, while those that don't will flush their money down the drain. Which circle would you like to travel in?

We Believe

- That everyone has the power to achieve their dreams and that they can accomplish what they set out to do once they have been shown how.

- That people gain power when they accept responsibility for their own destiny.

- That you're never too young or too old to understand how to make money and get rich.

- That entrepreneurship is accessible to all.

- That those who understand interest make it, and those that don't pay it.

- **That life insurance is solely for protection and virtually never as an investment.**

DID YOU KNOW

Experts agree, almost to the letter, on at least three things[2]. First, you must have an emergency fund. Second, buy a home, but only one that you can afford. And finally, don't forget life insurance, and that Term insurance is the answer for most people.

(2) New York Times, January 2016

Getting Rich

The following table illustrates the savings that can be made by simple changes in some common habits.

The Average Person VS the Rich Person.

Average Person	Rich Person	Saves over 30 Years
Cannot save extra money	Puts $50 per week into mutual funds paying ten per cent	$494,721.62
Pays minimum monthly on a $250,000, 30-year mortgage at 4.5 per cent	Pays extra $250 per month on mortgage	$65,944 and 7.5 years of payments
Pays minimum due on credit cards (average balance is $1,000 on all cards)	Pays off credit cards balance each month.	$7,525
Buys new wardrobe with unexpected $500 bonus	Invests bonus in mutual funds paying 10%	$82,247.01
Eats $10 lunch out twice every week	Limits eating out to one lunch (invests dollars saved at 10%)	$98,944.33
Smokes cigarettes, one pack per day	Quits smoking invests dollars saved at 7%	$298,591.29
Renews insurance policies automatically	Shops for the best car, home insurance	$8,200
Buys wrong kind of life insurance	Buys term and invests the difference	As we explain in Chapter 5 this can amount to millions
Pays late charges on bill payments	Pays bills on time	$3,700
Ignores suggestions to reduce heating or air conditioning costs by insulating home	Insulates home, turns off unused lights, installs thermostats, energy-efficient heater and light bulbs	$8,891
Pays full price on clothing	Buys clothes on sale (preseason or end of season sale)	$4,854
Total money saved		**$1,073,618.20**

Key # 1: Having the Right Attitudes About Getting Rich

> " A positive attitude causes a chain reaction of positive thoughts, events and outcomes. It is a catalyst and it sparks extraordinary results. "
>
> Wade Boggs

In our previous best-sellers, **The ABCs of Making Money** and **The ABCs of Making Money for Teens**, as well as in all our workshops, seminars and media appearances, we always start with the importance of *Attitudes*. What we learned, after interviewing several hundred self-made millionaires around the world, was that the formula for getting rich can be summed up in three words: Attitudes, Behaviors and Creations. Lots of people ask why Attitudes are so important. They just want to get to the parts where they learn to stop spending money needlessly and save more. "Can't I just skip to the Behaviors that will change my life?" The answer is: No, not if you want to be successful and stay that way. It's like beginning a fitness regimen. Everything is great for the first while until something comes up: you get really busy at work, or you do some traveling, and the fitness routine goes out the window.

It's the same with your financial life. You need to examine who you are and where you want to go before you start to integrate new Behaviors into your daily routine. Then, when a temptation threatens to drag you off course, you'll say, *Thanks, but no thanks. I have a much bigger goal I'm shooting for*.

⚠ Dangerous Attitudes

When we ask people about their beliefs on money, here are some of the responses we get:

- I could never get rich
- Money is evil
- Insurance is too confusing to ever understand
- Insurance is a great investment
- All insurance agents have my best interests at heart
- I could never run a successful business.

This is a great starting point. First, we repudiate all of the self limiting attitudes we just listed above and get people thinking about a much more powerful way of viewing wealth. The real problem with Attitudes is that they become self-fulfilling prophesies. This is true whether the Attitudes characterize feelings about money, work, or relationships. If you think you're going to fail, guess what: you will. If you think getting rich is something that only happens to other people, guess what: you will self-sabotage and create that reality.

One of the insurance stories we examined involved a smart man who, when confronted with the overwhelming evidence of an agent reducing his savings by two thirds, refused to believe it and continued using the agent as his adviser. Does that make any sense? He sabotaged himself out of a comfortable retirement.

So, what does wealth mean to you? Consider the meaning, and then write down your definition of being rich in the space below.

_____

_____

_____

Denis and Alan's definition of being rich:

"Having what you want, wanting what you have, and enjoying freedom".

Once you've examined your Attitude and eliminated anything that's holding you back, you need to identify some goals. And they should be realistic. Saving $10,000/month is a great goal, but if you are currently employed by a company paying you $1,000/month, the bigger goal really isn't achievable. So, what are your Goals?

_____

_____

As was said in *Alice in Wonderland*, "If you have no idea where you're going, any road will get you there." True. So here's a suggestion: figure out what you're passionate about and examine whether there's a way to make money from it. Let's say you love shopping. Could you hire out your services as a personal shopper for the time-starved executive? You love traveling, so you become a travel writer/blogger. You get the idea. Here's an exercise to help you connect with your passions.

What are you passionate about?

_____

_____

Getting Rich

If you were financially independent, how would you spend your time?

_____

_____

What would other people say is your greatest strength?

_____

_____

Who in history do you admire most, and why?

_____

_____

If you could solve a social problem or injustice, what would it be?

_____

_____

By identifying very clear and specific goals that are linked to what you're passionate about and supported by positive and realistic Attitudes about money, you're already well on your way to a very different financial future.

DID YOU KNOW

Why Set Wealth Goals?

You should set wealth goals for the following reasons:

- They force you to focus on the specific actions necessary to bring your wealth targets to fruition.
- They help you connect with your passions.
- They convert wishful thinking to reality.
- They hold you accountable for your own success.
- When opportunities present themselves, you are better equipped to recognize and act on them.
- They help you organize your daily activities for maximum benefit.
- They increase your odds of actually achieving your goals.

Ten Steps to Goal Setting

Consider the following ten steps in formulating your own financial goals:

1. State your getting rich goals in S.M.A.R.T. terms (that is, make them Specific, Measurable, Attainable, Realistic, and Timely).

2. Analyze your current situation relative to your goals.

3. Define why you want to achieve each goal, and how you will benefit from achieving it.

4. Identify the obstacles and challenges that you will have to overcome.

5. Identify the supportive people whose help you will need in achieving each goal.

6. Identify the knowledge and skills you will have to acquire or further develop to attain your goals.

7. Identify any attitudes you will have to change to achieve your goals.

8. Identify the visuals that can help you connect with achieving your goals.

9. Commit to taking specific steps toward achieve your goals.

10. Have your supportive person co-sign your goal sheet for additional accountability.

Now, with these ten steps firmly in mind, fill out the following table for each goal.

Getting Rich Goal Sheet	
The SMART getting rich goal that I will achieve is:	
It is Specific because:	
It is Measureable because:	
It is Attainable because:	
It is Realistic because:	
It is Timely because:	
My current situation relative to this goal is:	
I want to achieve this goal because:	
I have to overcome the following obstacles and challenges to achieve my goal:	
I need the assistance of the following people to achieve my goal:	
I need the following knowledge and skills to achieve my goal:	
The attitudes I need to change to achieve this goal are:	
The visuals I can use to help me connect with achieving this goal are:	
I commit to the following specific steps to achieve my goal:	
My Signature Supportive Person's Signature	

Many of us can relate to Australian Pam Brossman's story. She and her husband were employed with good jobs, were enjoying the middle class lifestyle, and had a nice home. Unfortunately, like millions of people, they were living beyond their means, and a bad investment led to a financial crisis. The Brossmans didn't just lose their house; they also had $30,000 in credit card debt and owed more than $80,000 to their families.

The sudden turn for the worse was devastating to Pam, who spent four years in a state of depression, obsessed with how stupid she had been and doubting her abilities. At one point her son asked her why she never asked people over to the apartment they had moved into after losing their house. After a bit of reflection, Pam realized that she was embarrassed by their current home, and that she had basically given up. That was the turning point; Pam didn't want her son to see her as a quitter. She immediately changed her attitude by accepting responsibility for poor financial decisions in the past, and made the commitment to learn from her mistakes and move forward.

Pam consciously changed her Attitude. In her own words, "I believe challenges in business and in life are just tests to see if you really want it or not. Those who do want it will persevere and keep going no matter what. Those who are just testing the waters will either give up or move onto other things." She continues to say, "I also believe that sometimes a setback can be the catalyst for something even better that you never would have explored if the setback had never occurred. These days I always look for the rainbow in every bad situation because I know from experience that eventually I will find the pot of gold just waiting to be discovered."

Pam and her husband decided to get very focused and change their financial reality. They transferred all their high interest credit card debt to one card with an interest-free six-month promotion." They destroyed their credit cards, and had daily chats to find ways to cut expenses and stay on target. The Brossmans paid off the entire $30,000 within six months, before the interest period kicked in. Pam had a passion for vintage designer clothes which she turned to her financial benefit by purchasing pieces from charity shops in the wealthiest part of the city, and then selling them on eBay. She taught herself how to effectively use social media and video marketing to rapidly expand her growing business.

Pam and her husband turned their financial situation around completely. Pam has shared her experiences and insights in doing so with hundreds of thousands of people by publishing ten best-selling books and holding numerous seminars. Pam and her family are now enjoying a six-bedroom beach house, with a pool and tennis court. They are living proof of the power of a positive attitude toward getting rich.

Key # 2: Getting Rich
by Living Within Your Means

> " Advertising is the art of convincing people to spend money they don't have for something they don't need, to impress people they don't know.
>
> Will Rogers "

All self-made rich people know the value of being disciplined in their personal spending habits. They understand the need to delay instant gratification in their personal spending. These people do not view saving as a painful process. Rather, they see saving simply as deferred spending. Successful people realize that their first financial goal should be to learn to live better and smarter with their existing income.

Have you ever wondered where all your money goes? You work hard, get paid, and before you know it, all your money has disappeared. Most of us have some sense of what we spend our money on, but only by doing a more detailed exploration can we pinpoint the exact places where savings can be made.

⚠ Living Beyond Your Means

Many people believe that the answer to all their financial problems is simply to have more money. We often hear an expression like, 'Everything would be better if I could only get a ten percent raise.' The problem with this is that most people continue overspending by 15% to 20% regardless of how many raises they actually get. They've never really learned the power of living within their means.

On the **Getting Rich Snapshot**, fill in the amount of money that comes into your household and the amount you pay for each expense listed. This tool may seem complex, but when you read it, you'll find it's really easy to complete. If you don't have to pay for electricity, for example, just skip it and move on. We've included just about every conceivable expense, so don't worry about missing something significant. For annual costs such as house repairs, take the total cost and divide it by twelve. If you don't know the exact number, make a good guess.

Getting Rich

Getting Rich Snapshot: Income

Month: _____ of 20_____

Monthly Sources of Income	Person #1	Person #2	Person #3	Total
Full-time job				
Part-time job # 1				
Part-time job # 2				
Business Income – Net				
Unemployment Benefits				
Compensation or Sick Benefits				
Investment Income				
Retirement Income Fund				
Pension				
Welfare Payment				
Child Tax Credit				
Alimony				
Loan Income				
Rental Income				
Other				
Total Available Money per Month				

Getting Rich Snapshot: Other Income

Month: _____ of 20_____

Other Available Sources of Money	Person #1	Person #2	Person #3	Total
Severance Pay				
Superannuation Payment				
Insurance Claim				
Legal Settlement				
Income Tax Return				
Cash in RRSP or IRA				
Advance on Wages or Contract				
Advance on Item Sold				
Sell Equity in House or Business				
Scholarship or Grant				
Barter				
Sell House, Car or Other Items				
Cash in Bonds				
Sell Stocks				
Other				
Total Other Available Sources of Money				

Getting Rich Snapshot: Accommodations Expenses

Month: _____ of 20_____

Monthly Expense Accommodations	Person #1	Person #2	Person #3	Total
Mortgage, Rent or Room and Board				
Property Taxes				
Repairs and Maintenance				
Improvements				
Home Insurance or Tenants Insurance				
Electricity				
Natural Gas				
Heating Oil				
Water				
Telephone				
Internet Connection				
Cable/ Satellite				
Sanitation				
Appliances Repair or Upgrade				
Other				
Subtotal Accommodations Expenses				

Getting Rich

Getting Rich Snapshot: Automobile Expenses

Month: _____ of 20_____

Monthly Expense Automobiles	Person #1	Person #2	Person #3	Total
Loan or Lease Payments				
Repairs and Maintenance				
Fuel and Oil				
Registration and Licensing				
Insurance				
Parking				
Other				
Subtotal Automobiles Expenses				

Getting Rich

Getting Rich Snapshot: Financial Expenses

Month: _____ of 20_____

Monthly Expense Financial	Person #1	Person #2	Person #3	Total
Savings				
Life, Health, Medical and Disability Insurance				
Investment Contributions				
IRA/RRSP Contributions				
Credit Card # 1				
Credit Card # 2				
Credit Card # 3				
Credit Card # 4				
Credit Card # 5				
Loan Payment				
Alimony or Child Support Payment				
Other				
Subtotal Financial Expenses				

Getting Rich Snapshot: Family and Personal Expenses

Month: _____ of 20_____

Monthly Expense Family and Personal	Person #1	Person #2	Person #3	Total
Groceries				
Eating Out				
Prescriptions, Vitamins and Natural Remedies				
Doctor, Dentist, Chiropractor and Natural Health Practitioner				
Clothing				
Laundry and Dry Cleaning				
School/University Supplies				
Entertainment				
Baby-sitters				
Day Care/After School Program				
Child Recreation Fees				
Allowances				
Tuition Fees/Course Costs				
Memberships				
Travel/ Vacation				
Pet Food and Care				
Beauty, Barber Shop, Toiletry and Cosmetics				
Gifts/ Donations				
Tithing				
Other				
Subtotal Family and Personal Expenses				
Total Monthly Expenses				

Now that you've filled out the Getting Rich Snapshots, get creative. Analyze all of the expenses and ask yourself whether you could reduce or live without some of them. Do you really need the mobile phone? Perhaps you do, but do you need unlimited talk time? Maybe a minimum plan would suffice just so you have service in emergencies, or when you're running late. You may save $20 to $30 per month. Do you need all of those cable channels? Maybe the basic plan would give you what you *really* need and encourage more reading or physical activity. Are you paying off credit card debts at 18 or 28 per cent? Get a basic credit card that allows you to transfer debts and start paying the lower amount. Or, using the money you saved, add it to the amount you pay each month and get rid of the debt quicker.

Did You Know

In October 2015, the New York Times reported that the three largest banks in the country made more than **$1 Billion in overdraft fees** in just the first three months of the year! Paying these fees is completely unnecessary. Here's a better idea: take the money you save by resolving to avoid all penalty fees, and buy shares in the banks instead.

Now, here's the most important part of this exercise. If you have your debts under control and you find additional savings, why not put that extra cash directly into an investment plan so that it starts to work for you?

Let's pause for a moment and reflect on what we just suggested. If you're able to simultaneously reduce your debt while contributing more to your investments, you will be adding dramatically to your net worth. Congratulations; you're well on your way to Getting Rich!

Having completed this exercise, it's time for the next step – understanding your day-to-day spending habits. Here is a powerful way to track your daily purchases and determine whether they are **needs** or **wants**. For the sake of clarity, we define a **need** as something that is a fundamental requirement, such as healthy food. By this measure, we would call snacks and junk food, **wants**. We included a sample of some daily expenses below. As you can see, **wants** expenses can add up quickly and represent a substantial loss of possible savings.

Weekly Wants vs. Needs Tracker Sample

Monday		
Item	**Need Expense**	**Want Expense**
Coffee & donut		$3.99
Gas	$30.00	
Newspaper		$1.00
Juice & muffin		$4.50
Milk, bread, fruit	$9.50	
Drinks after work		$22.50
Amount that could have been saved if the wants were eliminated: $ 31.99		

Make some copies of the Weekly Wants vs. Needs Tracker below and fill it in every night before you go to bed – it's much easier to remember if you do it every day – over the course of a week or more. These exercises work whether you earn $10,000 a year or $100,000 a year. **It's not about how much you make, it's how much you keep, and what you do with it that counts.**

Weekly Wants vs. Needs Tracker

Monday		
Item	**Need Expense**	**Want Expense**
Amount that could have been saved if the wants were eliminated $		

Tuesday		
Item	**Need Expense**	**Want Expense**
Amount that could have been saved if the wants were eliminated $		

Wednesday		
Item	**Need Expense**	**Want Expense**
Amount that could have been saved if the wants were eliminated $		

Getting Rich

Weekly Wants vs. Needs Tracker

Thursday		
Item	Need Expense	Want Expense
Amount that could have been saved if the wants were eliminated $		

Friday		
Item	Need Expense	Want Expense
Amount that could have been saved if the wants were eliminated $		

Saturday		
Item	Need Expense	Want Expense
Amount that could have been saved if the wants were eliminated $		

Sunday		
Item	Need Expense	Want Expense
Amount that could have been saved if the wants were eliminated $		

Key # 3 Understanding Insurance

> **For most people, the right type of life insurance can be summed up in a single word: Term.**
>
> www.smartmoney.com

Why should you buy insurance?

You would be smart to buy insurance if you own assets that are worth protecting, such as a house, a car, or your health. Buying insurance is optional, but if the roof over your head comes down on you, or your house/apartment is broken into, or it burns down in a fire and you're left with nothing or almost nothing, you're going wish you had taken out some insurance to pay the costs of replacement.

When it comes to driving a car, most states and provinces require you to buy at least the bare minimum liability insurance in order to protect not just you, but other motorists and pedestrians from you. The optional protection covers collision, fire and theft.

In America, families can have their entire life savings wiped out by medical emergencies. Medical insurance is thus a necessity. Beware of any company that says there is no need for a medical checkup when enrolling. If you've ever had even the smallest health concern in the past, you can almost guarantee that the company will refuse to pay your costs when you need it, citing "... an undisclosed prior medical condition" as the reason. They do so even though they said a medical checkup was unnecessary.

Did You Know

By definition, insurance is "something providing protection against a possible negative eventuality." Simply stated, insurance is a form of protection. **But, you should never confuse protection and investment. They are two entirely separate concepts.**

Different types of insurance

The huge variety of insurance products can be overwhelming to the consumer. The following list enumerates only a small sample of the various kinds of insurance on the market:

- Alien abduction insurance
- Aviation insurance
- Builder's risk insurance
- Business interruption insurance
- Computer insurance
- Contents insurance
- Credit insurance
- Crime insurance

- Cyber-Insurance
- Directors and officers liability insurance
- Earthquake insurance
- Flood insurance
- Health insurance
- Home insurance
- Key person insurance
- Kidnap and ransom insurance

- Landlords' insurance
- Lenders mortgage insurance
- Liability insurance
- Life Insurance
- Marine insurance
- Medical insurance
- Mortgage insurance
- Payment protection insurance
- Pension term assurance
- Pet insurance
- Pollution insurance
- Professional liability insurance
- Property insurance
- Protection and indemnity insurance
- Rent guarantee insurance
- Satellite insurance
- Savings Deposit Insurance
- Shipping insurance
- Terminal illness insurance
- Terrorism insurance
- Trade credit insurance
- Travel insurance
- Vehicle insurance
- Wage insurance
- War risk insurance
- Weather insurance
- Workers' compensation
- Zombie fund

Some of these are important, while some simply play on the fears of naïve people. We probably don't need to spend much time on Zombie, or Alien Abduction insurance, so we'll talk about some of the key products and what you want to be aware of.

A Different Kind of Car Insurance

Protection can come in many forms. Both of us live in Northern cities, where winters can be quite severe. Whether it's the snow or freezing rain, driving can be treacherous. To combat this, the department of highways are out 24/7 to clear the roads. Salt is most commonly used to melt the snow and ice not pushed aside by the snowplough. The biggest challenge with these salty surfaces is the corrosion of metal. Even cars with full body immersion in primer paint, will get rust. We both own quality German made cars, and we tend to keep them for longer than most other car owners. We obtain much more value and lower ownership costs that way. Some of our savings is due to our emphasis on maintenance. For instance, we have our cars rust protected with Krown each fall (and no, neither of us own shares in the company or will profit in any way by mentioning it). Even with brand-new cars, we invest in this annual process. It cost around $110 per car, which is about 30% more than most rust-protection competitors, but we have found it truly protected our cars from rust, which in turn protected our investment.

Several years ago Denis' younger daughter had a serious car accident with one of the family cars. Luckily, she was not hurt at all, but the car was damaged beyond repair and was written off. Because of the age and mileage of the car, the appraiser offered a payout of only $7,500. Denis challenged this offer, explaining that the mileage was mostly highway miles, that the car had been meticulously maintained, and that there was absolutely zero rust on it. He offered all of his receipts to prove his maintenance claims, including those showing that Krown Rust Protection had been applied like clockwork every year since he purchased the car out of the showroom. Confronted by this additional information, the appraiser revised his payout offer to $12,500 stating, "...the single biggest contributor to the increase in payout was the Krown treatment."

⚠ Credit Insurance

Credit insurance comes in many forms with the most common being mortgage, car loan and credit card. As you will quickly see by reading the next few pages we are not fans of this type of "protection." An important thing to bear in mind with credit insurance is that the insured person's policy goes to the underwriting department for inspection after they die. If the underwriters determine that the insured was actually "uninsurable" because of something like a pre-existing medical condition, the debt will not be paid off. Instead of the expected elimination of debt, the survivor receives only a refund of premiums, and is left still owing the balance of the debt.

Getting Rich

Mortgage Insurance

If you own a home with a mortgage, particularly if there is one primary income earner in the family, it's very smart to have some kind of insurance policy to protect you in the case of something tragic befalling the primary "breadwinner". To most people, losing a spouse is unimaginable, but to compound that with losing the family home is truly unthinkable.

Many banks and mortgage lenders "helpfully" include some kind of insurance right in the mortgage documents, with the monthly premiums blended into the cost of the mortgage. To avoid paying this insurance, you have to search through the document, uncheck the appropriate box, and then face the scorn of the lender, who looks at you as if you've completely lost your mind.

Pretty much every way you look at this insurance, it's a bad deal. It typically costs between 0.5% to 1% of the entire loan amount on an annual basis. On a $250,000 mortgage, that means that you would be paying as much as $2,500 a year, or $208.33 per month – assuming a 1% fee. Bear in mind that you will be paying a constant premium. Many years later, when you only owe $50,000, you're still paying the same premium as when you owed five times that amount. And if the "breadwinner" dies at that time, and the insurance company does decide to pay it off, they're only on the hook for the $50,000 you still owe. If, on the other hand, you had taken out a $250,000 Term life insurance policy when you purchased your house, the survivor in this scenario would receive $250,000. The survivor could then pay off the $50,000 due on the mortgage and pocket the remaining $200,000. Bear in mind that the monthly premium on a $250,000 Term life policy is only a fraction of what would cost through credit insurance.

Alternatively, you could have declined the mortgage insurance and invested that extra $208/month into accelerated mortgage payments, For a 30 year mortgage at 5% interest; this would save you $67,555 in interest over the life of the mortgage, and chop 7 years off your payment period.

On the plus side, mortgage insurance is really easy to get because there are no supplemental credit or health checks. Such supplemental conditions are always an issue because, as mentioned, lenders have been known to renege on paying out the remaining mortgage because of undisclosed pre-existing conditions. Buried in the fine print when you sign a mortgage are the assumptions that you were in perfect health at the time of purchase. So, for example, if you neglected to mention that you had or have high blood pressure, that could very well be an obstacle to your widowed spouse collecting on the policy and staying in the home. It doesn't matter that you were never asked anything relating to your health at signing. Again, if you'd bought a Term life insurance policy, they'd be much more likely to ask you the prequalifying health questions.

Credit Card Insurance

This one is pretty simple. If you're carrying a balance on a credit card, DON'T. If they offer to sell you Credit Balance Insurance, don't add insult to injury; say "NO." It is much smarter to take that extra insurance fee to pay off your balance. Carrying a balance already means that you're paying excessive rates and fees. The smartest thing you can do is pay that amount off completely and as rapidly as possible. Some clever people transfer all their balances to one card that offers them a really low rate for six months, and then make sure that the entire balance is paid off before the end of the period and cut up all of their cards!

Loan and Car Loan Insurance

This is pretty much the same as the other "credit" insurances. You should think of any credit insurance as a tax on the outstanding amount, a tax that only slows you down from paying it all off. Don't fall prey to the paranoia they're selling you; concentrate instead on paying off your debts as quickly as possible.

Extended Warranties

Most of these warranties are a waste of money. Most products come with at least a 90 day, or a one year, warranty. If that product is going to fail, 90% of the time it will fail within that time period. If it hasn't failed over that first period, chances are it won't for a couple of years, at which point you're probably ready for the updated model anyway. This is particularly true for most electronics.

DID YOU KNOW

Another consideration is to buy high quality goods in the first place. When something is really inexpensive, you really ought to wonder why. Products from companies like BMW or Apple, to name just two companies with sterling reputations, are really well designed and built. They'll likely outlast their competitors. They may cost a little more, but if you get twice the average lifespan, then you really paid less.

Key # 4: Determine How Much Protection You Need

> As a quick rule of thumb, people should buy enough life insurance to equal **five to 10 times** their annual income.
>
> Post-Gazette

DID YOU KNOW

We don't all need life insurance throughout our entire lives, any more than we need auto or homeowners' insurance. If you no longer drive a car, you don't need auto insurance. If you no longer own a home, you don't need homeowners' insurance. In certain circumstances, you may no longer need life insurance. One such circumstances is when you and your spouse have accumulated enough assets and income streams to independently care for yourselves. Another might be when your children are self-sufficient adults. Yet another might be when your estate is too small to owe estate taxes, or is liquid enough to pay the taxes.

Model of Changing Needs

The core concept behind *The Model of Changing Needs* has been around for decades; in our opinion, it is still valid, and still worthy of working towards. Under this concept, the need for income protection changes as a family evolves and gradually gets its financial affairs in line (by using strategies such as the ones we suggest). Younger families with dependents typically require more income protection (life insurance) for the income earner(s). As the family grows older, the need for income protection usually declines. If you've saved and invested wisely, as we recommend in this book, you should have a significant amount of accumulated cash to enjoy in your retirement years. In this case you have in effect become "self-insured," and eliminated your need for life insurance. However, there are people today in their 60s and 70s with responsibilities for dependents (adult children, parents, grandchildren), as well as some seniors who are carrying heavy debt loads including mortgage balances. There are a host of reasons for these financial realities ranging from unforeseen circumstances, to excessive consumerism, and poor financial planning. For people in this situation, we understand that carrying these burdens comes with a tremendous amount of stress, which needs to be eliminated. We strongly recommend that you read this entire book, and consider reading *The ABCs of Making Money*, in which we provide more in-depth strategies to reduce expenses, accelerate debt elimination, and make various investments that yield multiple sources of passive income. We are so passionate about sharing financial literacy across North America that 10 years ago we wrote *The ABCs of Making Money for Teens*, and developed a series of free workshops as a proactive measure to keep the upcoming generation from falling into dangerous financial traps.

Consider the model on the next page as it depicts the changing needs of a family over time.

EARLY YEARS   **RETIREMENT YEARS**

Income Protection Needed

- Young Children
- High Debt
- Mortgage

Retirement Income Needed

- Independent Children
- Low/no debt
- No mortgage

DID YOU KNOW

**Nearly one-third of Americans said they
needed more life insurance in 2015.**

Life Insurance and Market Research Association

The SAFE Method of Determining Your Essential Income Protection Needs

Estimating your true life insurance needs can seem like a daunting task. We recommend that people use our simple system to determine their life insurance needs. We call it the **SAFE Method** because it's all about safety and income protection for your family. The key is to get enough protection without buying too much. The basic elements addressed by our **SAFE Method** are as follows:

- **S**tyle of life that you wish to maintain;
- **A**ssets currently owned that can contribute towards future needs;
- **F**inancial obligations of major expenses;
- **E**ssential income protection needed.

To obtain the information needed for the SAFE analysis, go back to pages 23 -28 and review the **Getting Rich Snapshots.**

Style of life that you wish to maintain is calculated by adding up:		
Monthly Expenses	**Total**	**Notes**
Accommodations		
Automobiles		
Financial		
Family and Personal		
Total Monthly Expenses		A
Total Monthly Expenses (A) x 12 months = Yearly Amount (B)		B
Estimate the # of years income that would be needed for survivors multiplied by (B) = (C)		C

Assets currently owned is calculated by adding up:

Assets	Total	Notes
Cash and savings		
Partner's after tax annual income x # working years.		
Non tax sheltered stocks, bonds & mutual funds		
Tax sheltered investments net value after tax		
Real estate		
Business assets		
Other assets		
Total assets		D

Financial obligations of major expenses is calculated by adding up:

Obligations	Total	Notes
Pay out balance of mortgage		
Pay out balance of all credit cards		
Pay of balance of all other loans		
Final expenses (burial, probate, tax, executor fees)		
Child-care expenses		
Children education		
Bequests		
Other obligations		
Total obligations		E

Essential income protection needed is calculated by:

Step 1: Insert amount from calculation (C) above $ _____

Step 2: Subtract total assets (D) from (C) $ _____

Step 3: Add total obligations (E) $ _____

Total essential income protection needed $ _____

Note: This is the amount of Term life insurance coverage you require!

If you are in a hurry to determine your approximate income protection needs consider the "10X Rule of Thumb". Take your annual gross salary and multiple it by 10, that number represents a quick estimate of your Term insurance needs.

Now that you know how much life insurance to get, make sure that your family is properly protected by obtaining this amount of coverage with a Term life policy from a competitively priced, reputable insurance provider. Whatever coverage you choose, buy only one policy, and put the entire coverage amount on that policy. Separate policies mean separate fees and will cost more! Prior to shopping for any life insurance, please make sure you read the follow chapter.

DID YOU KNOW

According to a 2015 LIMRA study, 65 percent of Americans said they had not purchased more life insurance because they thought it was too expensive, and 80 percent of consumers misjudged the price of Term life insurance.

Remeber life insurance is two things:

1. A bet that you hope to lose, because if you win you are dead.
2. It is "renting wealth" until you can afford to get your own.

In conclusion, we strongly encourage our readers to heed the following advice:

> I strongly believe that Term is the best insurance for the vast majority of people, and it literally **costs a fraction** of all other forms of life insurance.
>
> Suze Orman

Key # 5 Avoid Life Insurance Rip-offs

> " Cash value life insurance is one of the
> worst financial products available.
>
> Dave Ramsey "

⚠ Life Insurance Rip-Off

How would you like to buy into a savings plan in which you invest $1000/month, but your balance stays at zero for 2-5 years? Then, when you've eventually saved up a balance, we allow you to borrow some of what you've saved - but with an interest rate you don't control, something in the vicinity of 7%. And, if you die, we will pay your beneficiary an agreed-upon lump sum, and keep whatever you've saved over all those years for ourselves. Sadly, this is typical of what most Whole life policies are offering.

DID YOU KNOW

The North American insurance industry has assets of around $7 Trillion. Life insurance premiums alone amounted to $190 Billion in 2014. With that kind of financial clout, it's not entirely unimaginable that they, as an industry, could afford to hire some lobbyists, and mount some persuasive public campaigns to protect their positions.

In fact, The Federal Trade Commission Improvements Act of 1980 actually **prohibits any future investigations** of the "business of insurance" by the Commission. Really???

During the course of our research for this book we met several strong advocates for Whole and Universal life policies. While there may be a place for these policies in certain unusual circumstances, we believe that such cases are NOT the norm, and do not apply to most consumers. The "pro" side of the argument usually turns on the permanent aspect of this insurance, which may be useful under circumstances such as a pre-existing medical condition, or providing for a disabled child. Our biggest problem has always been with the investment value of these policies.

None of the advocates for Cash value policies argued that their returns were better than what they would have received through a low fee investment account. Insurance companies are by nature conservative, and their commissions and fees, very high. In all the cases we looked at (which are covered later in this chapter), those fees ate up virtually the entire investment.

Fees

We have always warned clients about the dangers of high fees. For example, paying an annual 2% management fee (MER) instead of a 1% fee can have a huge negative impact on a portfolio over a 30-year period. Having said that, we would both happily pay a 3% MER if a fund was consistently returning, say, 15% annually. That doesn't happen very often. Most non-insurance mutual funds and ETFs express their annual returns net of all fees so that you can compare the return of the funds based on their performance. New rules and consumer demand are bringing down the MERs of many funds, but be aware that those fees may appear elsewhere on your account. Some firms are "lowering" their fees but adding "statement preparation charges" or "annual account fees" to customer's statements. That's because these charges are not regulated and aren't counted in the fund's MER. If this happens to you, complain. Loudly. Threaten to close your account if they don't remove the charge – the worst they can say is "No."

If a Cash value salesperson promises a 3% return (minus fees) on a policy, the first thing you need to know, apart from the fact that he is probably exaggerating, is that there are no guarantees with Universal life policies, just as there are no guarantees with any equities, mutual funds or ETFs. Secondly, the difference between an insurance portfolio returning 3% after 30 years ($289,865 **before** deducting fees) does not even compare to one returning 6% ($492,106 **after** all fees are deducted), which is reasonably common these days.

⚠ Complicated = Costly

"And so it is with life insurance, where the simplest solution — Term insurance — is usually the best...sales agents, however, are often eager to push other forms of insurance that include complex investments, large and often hidden fees, and complex riders laden with mumbo jumbo[1]."

It is important to note that no product is perfect for everyone, and in theory ALL products are perfect for at least someone. Moreover, there are exceptions to every rule. That being said, what you need to know is that for 98+% of all North Americans, **anything other than Term insurance is a rip-off**. As we mentioned earlier, we have examined a tremendous amount of Whole and Universal life policies, and were shocked by what we saw. **Life insurance – under almost all circumstances – is not an investment tool.**

Our friend Hector in Los Angeles shared a story about a young guy who bought a Cash Value policy several years ago when he was 22. The policy gave him $50,000 worth of protection for a $50/month premium, and when he reached his 65th birthday he would get a payout of $28,000. Maybe. Several years later he was offered a Term policy which gave him $250,000 worth of coverage for only $30/month. So, he got five times the coverage, for $20 less/month. True, he lost out on the $28,000 retirement present, but if he had invested that $20/month he saved in a low fee fund returning an average 10% over those 42 years, **he would have ended up with $166,768**. We know which option we'd take.

(1) New York Times, Jan 8, 2016

We'll get to some more real life examples shortly, but first let's go back and establish some terms of reference.

Glossary of Insurance Terms

Beneficiary - an individual who will receive payment from a life insurance policy.

Cash Value Life Insurance – A category of insurance products including: Universal life, Whole life, and Variable life insurance, They may contain benefits in addition to a death benefit, such as dividends, interest, or cash value available for a loan, or upon surrender of the policy. None of these returns are guaranteed for Universal or Variable life policies.

> **Whole Life** - Life insurance that may be kept in force for a person's entire, or "Whole," life, which pays a benefit upon the person's death. Part of each premium payment will go into cash value (the investment), another part for the death benefit, and yet another part for expenses like commissions and administrative costs. You have no control over how the money is invested in the policy.

> **Permanent Insurance** – Life insurance designed to provide protection until the insured's death or until a specified date.

> **Variable Life insurance** – This is a hybrid of permanent life insurance and an investment. The cash value (the investment component) – which is not guaranteed – is invested in equities, T-Bills, bonds, and money market funds. The premiums are said to be guaranteed but will actually fluctuate due to investment yields, and the death benefit varies with performance of the investments.

> **Universal Life (UL)** - Policies in which premiums and coverage are adjustable. It has extra options as compared to Whole Life but it comes with high surrender charges, particularly in the 1st to 10th years, during which time the client usually cannot access any of their deposits.

Index Universal Life (IUL) - Combines insurance with investments mirroring the activity in selected Index funds. If the Index goes up, you get a piece of the returns. If it goes down, you're protected. Sounds great. Except that you only get a **piece** of the returns; you get none of the dividends the Index generates; there's a cap on how much you can gain, plus you pay the usual fees and commissions.

Death benefit - Amount paid to the beneficiary upon the death of the insured.

Dividend – Should not be confused with a share of profits from a company listed on a stock exchange. In insurance terms, it is a refund to the insured of a portion of premiums that were overpaid. Policy dividends are not guaranteed, and may be increased or decreased at the discretion of the company.

Policy Loan – A loan made by a life insurance company to a policy owner based on the security of the cash value of their policy.

Premium - The amount the life insurance company collects per unit time to keep the policy in force.

Surrender charges - Charges that are deducted if a life insurance policy or annuity is cashed in (surrendered). These charges also are deducted if the policyholder borrows money on the policy, or if the policy lapses for non-payment.

Term – The period of time for which policy is in effect.

Term Insurance - Life insurance payable only if the death of the insured occurs within a specified time, such as 5, 10, 20, 30 or 40 years, or before a specified age.

Underwriting – The process by which a life insurer determines whether, or on what basis, it will accept an application for insurance payout. If a claim is denied, it's likely that it was disqualified by this department. Disqualification often occurs after many years of the company's accepting your payments.

The Vanishing Premium

Between 1980 and 1995, insurance companies sold policies on the basis that, after a certain period of time (12 years on average), the customer would no longer have to pay premiums. This was because part of the monthly premium was considered an investment, which accrued dividends. The dividends would eventually pay the premiums. Sounds great. Unfortunately, not all policyholders realized that their monthly premiums would triple over the course of the 12-year payment period. But when interest rates fell so far that insurance companies could not afford to eliminate the premiums on these policies, they tried to get away with merely reducing, instead of eliminating, the monthly premiums. Not surprisingly, this move was followed by a number of class action lawsuits[2].

DID YOU KNOW

"A recent **Forbes Helpline** caller said that she was quoted an annual premium of about $8,700 for a permanent (Cash value) policy. She could purchase the same amount of Term insurance for 30 years for only about $700 a year. If the investments in the permanent policy earned 8% over 30 years, it was projected to grow after expenses to about $600,000, some of which could be borrowed tax-free. That sounds great but investing the $8,000 difference in a Roth 401(k) with the same 8% return (but without the higher expenses) would provide her about $980,000, all tax-free after 30 years. Quite frankly, **the Cash value policy robbed her of an extra $380,000** that might have gone toward her becoming wealthy."

(2) Lawsuits Launched Against Insurers-National Post

DID YOU KNOW

In 2015, the *Wall Street Journal* noted that, after the 2008-09 financial crisis, sales of Whole life policies "spiked," with people abandoning what they perceived as a risky stock market for presumably more stable insurance plans. **"Yet many of the policies still have the same issues they always have had: often-steep agent commissions, high cancellation rates, and annual costs that can be both high and difficult to understand."**

Paying the high premiums Whole life policies demand was more than many could afford. As a result, "… the Society of Actuaries found that 20% of Whole life policies are terminated in the first three years, and 39% within the first 10 years." Another reason, besides high premiums, that so many policies were terminated was the fact that, after 3 years of paying high premiums, some people actually read their statements and discovered that they had absolutely nothing to show for their "investments."

The "favorable" tax position is also an interesting twist. As we've said, real dividends are profits from companies paid out to shareholders after the company has paid all their taxes. So, they're taxed at a lower rate. When "dividends" come from insurance policies, they aren't actually dividends, but rebates from the premiums you've overpaid. You don't pay taxes, because they're just giving you back a portion of your own money.

James Hunt is an actuary at the Consumer Federation of America. He says, "Cash-value policies are impossible for laypersons to penetrate. Costs can go up, and dividends can go down." Brian Fechtel, an agent quoted by the *Wall Street Journal* notes that, "In their pitches, agents typically use 'illustrations' to project the cash-value account's growth over time." He describes these illustrations as "fanciful sheets of numbers," because there is no certainty they will be realized.

⚠ Exaggerated Projections

In 2002, Rick Stoutley, a sales director at the giant AIG Life, cautioned salespeople to, "temper the 'illustrations' used to sell clients."[3] Stoutley had seen agents' projections of client returns that were twice as large as realistic estimates. He then went on to suggest that **"agents protect themselves by not leaving hard copies of their illustrations with clients."**

Corey, an agent we spoke with in Vancouver, explained that there are four rules of thumb governing all Cash Value policies:

1. From year 1 to 4, your "investment" will have $0.00 dollars available in it, even though your policy statement may say otherwise, unless the policy is heavily funded with cash when it's set up.

2. You will virtually never get more than 1 to 2% in returns, and that's before all fees and deductions are paid. And, if you ever withdraw your "investments" the insurance policy will terminate.

3. The insurer will charge you a hefty interest rate to *borrow your own money.*

(3) National Post, 2002

4. If you die, your estate/beneficiary will get the death benefit, but the cash value you've built up will be deducted from the death benefit. And, if you have borrowed any of your own money, that (plus any interest) will also be deducted from the death benefit before it's paid.

Universal Life

This is sold as the Rolls Royce of life insurance policies. It promises to give you everything: a death benefit, an investment, and a tax shelter. But at the end of the day, it's probably the agent who will be driving the fancy car, not you. In fact you'll probably still be taking a bus.

The catch here is that your "savings" or your "investment" is subject to deductions for commissions, fees and "Surrender Charges" which, as we'll see, can eat up hundreds of thousands of your dollars.

Unfortunately, as we've said, there is a history of questionable practices in the industry dating back decades (see comments in the *Wall Street Journal* and *National Post* cited previously). Our caution to you is: if someone is trying to sell you on the investment potential of an insurance policy, note whether they leave their "investment projections" behind. It would be reassuring if the agent would sign a guarantee as to how well your investment will perform. If they don't, then just say "No."

The essence of what we have suggested in this book is that you should cultivate the right Attitudes, set meaningful goals, live within your means, avoid common insurance rip-offs, and invest the money you save wisely outside of an insurance policy. There are an overwhelming number of good, relatively safe investment options. The insurance industry has its own "investment" products but their returns are almost always inferior, and suffer from high fees and commissions.

What the Bold Print Giveth, the Fine Print Taketh Away

We first heard this phrase from Bob, a good friend of ours in Calgary, and a tireless campaigner against Cash value policies. It perfectly captures one of the biggest problems with most insurance policies: their size and complexity. Policies which were once an average of 11 pages are now around 100 pages. We recently saw one that was 107. They are written in arcane legalese that is designed to confuse and overwhelm the client, who therefore must depend on the "kindness" of the "friendly neighborhood" agent. Unfortunately, 98% of agents themselves don't entirely understand how Universal life policies work[4]. This is just as well (we will give them the benefit of doubt here); they wouldn't sleep very well if they did. Add to that the fact that 99% of clients do not read all of the fine print. If they did, they'd see what was really going to happen to their "investment." If your so called "friend/agent" wanted what was best for you they would have advised you to get Term insurance right from the start. If they didn't, then it's time to get a new agent.

(4) National Post 2/04/2002

Index Universal Life

Index Universal Life (IUL) is the latest wrinkle in Cash Value policies. It combines a permanent death benefit with the current trend of Index investing. As usual, the devil is in the details. As Investopedia says: "IULs are considered advanced life insurance products in that they can be difficult to adequately explain and understand." This is another example of an instrument that was designed to be more successful for the salesperson than the purchaser.

The way it works is that part of your monthly premium goes toward the death benefit, part goes to paying fees and commissions, and if there's anything left, it goes into a cash value account which rises in proportion to the gain of an Index fund the purchaser selects. So, if you select an Index such as the S&P 500, and it increases by 5% over a selected period of time, your cash value account goes up by 5%. At least, in theory. Unfortunately, any gains are subject to a "**Participation rate**" which is set by the insurance company. If your participation rate is 25% (it *could* be higher), then you only get 25% of that 5% gain. In fairness, if the Index drops by 5% your account is not penalized. But, there are also **"Cap rates"** which put an upper limit on how much you can gain. If your selected Index went up by 26%, as the S&P did in 2009, your piece of the profits is capped at somewhere between 10–15%, then subject to your participation rate. Our advice: STAY AWAY! FAR AWAY!

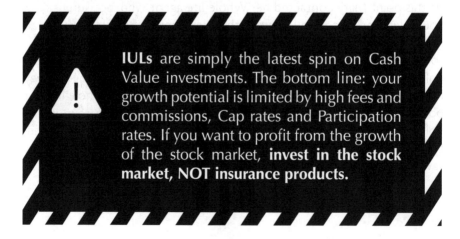

IULs are simply the latest spin on Cash Value investments. The bottom line: your growth potential is limited by high fees and commissions, Cap rates and Participation rates. If you want to profit from the growth of the stock market, **invest in the stock market, NOT insurance products.**

Examples of Real Life People Who Were Ripped-Off

(Due to space constraints we are unable to reproduce copies of the following policies. We do, however, keep copies of all of them in our offices and are happy to share them with media or investigators.)

Example 1: Mary

In 2011, a 42 year old single woman we'll call Mary, was looking for a tax efficient savings plan for her retirement. She had no children, so she had no need for life insurance, but an agent convinced her that her best option was to buy a Whole life policy with a death benefit of $299,000. Four years later, she had made premium payments that totaled $33,000. The good news was that if she died, her estate would now get $301,000.

In 2015, Mary met a Term life agent who asked to review her plan. He showed her that her plan wasn't worth quite what she thought it was, and suggested that she dump it. At first, Mary was a little skeptical about cancelling the policy. One of the things she had liked about it was that she could borrow money and use it for whatever she wanted. But when the agent showed her that after four years of faithfully making her $750/month payments, she could only borrow a maximum of $466, she was shocked. And, to add insult to injury, if she did borrow that $466, she would have to pay an interest rate of 7.5%. For her own money!

At this point Mary contacted her Whole life agent who, not surprisingly, counseled her to continue paying the premiums at all costs. Mary read her latest statement a little more closely, and found that if she wanted to cash out of her policy, after $33,000 worth of payments, she would only get $1,077. In other words, almost $32,000 of her hard-earned money had disappeared. As our friend Bob once said, "If you had a hole in your pocket, would you keep putting money in it or would you sew up the hole?" Mary cancelled her policy. And, to pour more salt on the wound, the company deducted the next two $750 premium payments from her savings of $1,077, leaving her with absolutely nothing.

Mary was understandably angry but there was nothing she could do. She considered suing the company but, first of all, she was not in the financial position to be going up against a multi-billion dollar company with an in-house army of well-paid lawyers. Secondly, she had signed a contract. It's not the company's fault that she didn't read the 17 pages of fine print it contained. It probably didn't help her mood when the Term salesman explained that if she did have an actual need for life insurance, she could have bought a 30-year, level Term policy instead of the Whole life policy, and would have been paying $82/month in premiums instead of $750. And, we figure, if she'd invested the remaining $668/month at an average 8% return, she would have had $36,000 at that same point in 2015 instead of $0, and $960,893 at the end of the 30 years. Ouch.

Focus on the Facts

If you have one of these policies, understand that **both Variable and Universal life are sold by illustration. The best thing to do is to ignore the illustration and get an updated annual statement and read it carefully**. If you don't understand all the terms, ask for an explanation. Don't talk to the agent, instead call the insurance company head office and inquire about the savings. After all, it's your money. Better yet, find a Term only insurance salesperson and get a second opinion.

> **If you need life insurance, get Term insurance. If you want to invest for retirement, invest in IRA's, 401K's, or similar retirement plans.**
>
> CNN Money

Example 2: Cary

A man we'll call Cary, is a 61-year-old who owns a large company. Four years ago he decided that it was in his company's best interest to have a life insurance policy on him. That way, if he died, the company would have some funds to carry on and transition to new management. He was also interested in setting up a tax efficient investment using some of the company profits.

Cary was approached by a Universal life salesman who decided that what Cary needed was a very sophisticated kind of policy, one that only elite business people, such as himself, could understand. It was full of tax efficiencies, estate planning considerations, and other things that would make your head spin, as well as a death benefit of $3.7 million. How the salesman came up with that figure is a mystery. Our guess is that the resulting commission equaled what the salesman needed to buy a new car, or a down payment on a house or condo.

The actual cost of the insurance policy was $2,517/month (at the time of the policy summary we reviewed), which was already $300/month more expensive than it was when the policy started in 2010. The premium would continue to rise as Cary got older, even though the death benefit would remain the same. Like many, Cary assumed that because he had a "Level Premium," the cost of his insurance would also remain constant. Not so much. The insurance portion of a Universal life policy is renewable every year, which means the cost of the insurance goes up every year inside the policy. This is why you want to have something called "Level Cost of Insurance" in any good policy. As we looked at the policy statement, we noticed that the "Floor Face Amount" was $936,400. It's anyone's guess (we asked several agents) whether the company would have paid the $3.7 million or the $936,400 if Cary had died, because the policy said, "Minimization of the face amount after 5 years".

The $2,517 figure was just the beginning of Cary's payments. When the investment portion of the policy was included, monthly premiums rose to $5,749. However, for reasons no agent who reviewed this policy could determine, Cary's company was actually paying an extra $3,308/month on top of the $5,749, for a total of **$9,058/month**. (The most likely reason for this extra premium was to add funds to the investment portion of the policy......or the commissions).

After four years of dutifully making payments, Cary was urged by a knowledgeable friend, who was licensed in the insurance industry, to show him a copy of the same statement that we examined. At that point (2014), Cary's policy was, theoretically, worth $355,201.

Eleven months later, when the up-to-date statement was printed, we noted that Cary's company had now made a total of $434,790 in payments. But that was not the balance. Deducted from that figure was the rather high cost of the insurance, which had risen over the past 11 months from $27,696 to $30,215/year, for a total $108,375 paid to date. Then, $8,695 in tax payments was also deducted – so much for tax efficiency. Moreover, $36,141 was deducted for "Interest" because, apparently, the amount of the investment had gone down. Other costs brought the balance down to $318,110.

On the positive side, Cary's company had earned a mighty $624 in interest. At the end of the day, after $434,790 in payments, the policy was worth $318,110. Theoretically. But not really.

If Cary's company decided that their investment wasn't working out in their favor, they could stop paying the premiums and get their $318,110 back, right? Sorry. If they stop paying and cancel the policy, **they will** have to pay a "Surrender Charge" - mostly representing commissions which have already been paid to the sales agent - of $206,976. This would leave Cary's company with only $111,108.

Now, if we had invested $434,790 and found out that all we had to show for it was $111,108 – even considering that about a quarter of that $434,790 amount had gone to the cost of the insurance – we would be very upset. Cary certainly was. He called up his original agent, who explained that everything Cary's friend was showing him – on the insurer's own print out – was being misinterpreted. Then, partly in shock, partly out of embarrassment, Cary stopped taking his friend's calls.

As we looked through the breakdown of the Investment funds in the policy, we could see part of the problem: two of the funds mentioned in Cary's portfolio didn't exist at the listed investment company. They didn't have an "Emerging Markets EMT 080 001 certificate" fund, or a "Global Stocks GEM 080 001 certificate" fund. It's probably just as well, seeing as how they, apparently, had lost $39,355 in the preceding 11 months.

Example 3: Sharon

Sharon had really nice grandparents. They were successful and wanted to share their good fortune with her and their 3 great-grandchildren (aged 10, 12 and 17 years at the time). Because Sharon's grandfather was not a big fan of paying taxes, he called up his long-time financial adviser and asked for some tax efficient trust funds for his grandchildren: $50,000 for each, plus $30,000 for Sharon to administer the funds, and $125,000 to help pay for the children's education.

The adviser, a very likable guy that you'd be happy to have at a family function, seemed beyond trustworthy. Whatever he suggested was fine with everybody. He decided that he would insure the lives of each of the children for between $750,000 and $1million. Now, to insure children for that kind of sum is insane. From a purely financial perspective, children have no monetary value: they don't earn money, and they also don't have any dependents. If something tragic happens, you only need the cost of the funeral and some counseling for you and your spouse. That's not going to amount to $1million. In fact, there is a chilling term for this type of excessive coverage: it's called "Blood Money," because the only reason to take out such a policy is either to pay a huge commission to the sales agent, or because you harbor ill intentions toward your kids.

If a family is in a situation where it would need to borrow money to pay for the funeral costs of their child, then we would recommend that the parents simply add a $10,000-$15,000 child rider onto their existing "Parents" policy.

The agent put most of the money ($180,000) into **four Universal life policies, which invested the money in a 0% daily interest savings plan**. Wait. What? As we were listening to this story we had to stop her and say, "Could we back up a bit; we think we missed something." The response we got was, "No, you heard correctly."

Sharon and her grandfather had no idea what the adviser had done. They assumed he had put all the money into some kind of mutual funds that would appreciate nicely over the years. Hardly.

Five years later, Sharon was introduced to an agent selling Term life and other investment plans. She asked Sharon if she could have a look at the investment to see how it was doing. Sharon was shocked at what she found. After five years, the $305,000 original investment was now worth $180,000. Not surprisingly, Sharon was mad. She felt betrayed and wanted out of the "investments." Unfortunately, **cancelling the insurance policy cost her $76,000 in Surrender Fees**. Not a great return.

DID YOU KNOW

After hearing Sharon's horror story, we couldn't resist doing a couple of "What if" scenarios:

First, if the agent had invested the $50,000 per child in separate growth funds returning 7%, and absolutely nothing more had been added over the years, **each child would have had $1,472,851** when they hit early retirement age.

Second, if he had invested the $180,000 into the S&P 500 – instead of the four UL policies – that part of the investment would now be worth $402,809, even considering all the ups, downs and meltdowns in the market in the 16 years between 1999 and 2015, (the year of our interview). And, if he had invested the whole amount, as the client expected, the S&P stock roller coaster ride would have turned the $305,000 into $727,454 (before taxes) over those 16 years.

When a customer realizes that they've made a horrendous investment, they typically cash out immediately, and have little if any money left to show for their "investment." They are in no position to challenge the might of the insurance company's legal team. And even if they did, they would find out that the company is protected by the provisions of the contract's fine print.

After reading these stories the first question likely to come to mind is: *What about my policy?* If you think that you have something that is in any way similar to any of the examples just presented, you need a second opinion on your policy from a trusted Term life representative. He or she will set up a face-to-face meeting with you to determine your financial goals, review your current situation, and customize a financial roadmap uniquely suited to you and your family.

DID YOU KNOW

Looking at the current options, one company that we have found that has the conviction and discipline to offer only Term life insurance policies is **Primerica**. In our experience, they offer straightforward financial advice without any tricks or "gotcha's." It has a proud history of serving American and Canadian families for almost 40 years. Currently there are approximately 100,000 field representatives educating families how to live within their means, and to *"buy term and invest the difference"*. Their motto, "We do what is right 100% of the time by always putting the client first," means that they educate the consumer to understand what they are getting, and what they need, so they can make an informed decision based on what is right for them.

Note: In the spirit of full disclosure, the authors have spoken at many of the company's field leaders' events. However, the authors have never been representatives of Primerica, never received any money to promote the company, and have never owned any Primerica stock.

If you found the preceding stories upsetting, you may be asking yourself several questions. One question might be; how is it possible to sell such policies in the first place? **The reality is that it's just too lucrative for the salesperson to sell anything other than Whole or Universal life.** The sales rep will usually receive between 5 to 10 times the commission compared to what they would get if they were selling a Term life policy. This is part of a 200 year history of doing business in a certain way. Anecdotally, we've heard that most insurance companies will fire salespeople who sell too much Term insurance.

Another common question might be: why are these well-known companies allowed to get away with this while maintaining an "A" rating? They can because, essentially, you signed the contract. The agent may have misrepresented the outcome, but you signed it. And you probably didn't read the pages and pages of fine print before you signed it. So, according to the letter of the law, the company did nothing illegal. Immoral and unethical, yes; but that's another issue.

Are there examples of Cash value policies in which the client was treated better? Possibly, but as of today, we just haven't seen one. If you have had a positive experience with one of these, please get in touch so that we can add your example to a future update. In the meantime, after looking at the real life examples we have presented, ask yourself whether any of these situations mirror your own experience. If you are that one-in-a-hundred who requires a permanent life insurance policy, understand what you're sacrificing on the investment side. For everyone else, you probably just want to take a pass.

How to Move Forward

If, after reviewing your financial situation with a skilled financial professional, you come to the conclusion that you wish to cancel your current life insurance policy, but are unsure where to start, you need to inform your current insurance company of your intention. Fred, a good friend of ours who lives in Kingston, and has been in the insurance industry for over 20 years, has kindly shared a template letter that you can use. We present that letter on page 69 and we recommend it **be sent by registered mail:**

Maintain Your Protection

Don't cancel any permanent life insurance policy until you have a Term life policy in place!

Template for Cancelling a Life Insurance Policy

To: (Name of Life Insurance Company)

       (Complete address of Life Insurance Company)

Date:

From: (Your Name)

       (Your Address)

Subject: **LETTER OF DIRECTION**

Reference: Life Insurance Policy #XXXXXXXXXXXXXXXXXXXXXXX

Please accept this letter of direction to:

1. Cancel the above referenced policy effective the date of this letter;
2. Return any applicable Cash Values or Dividends due to me; and
3. Mail the check (if applicable) to my address as stated above.

Sincerely,

Signature   Signature

_____   _____

(Print Policy Owners Name)   Witness

If you choose to take this step and replace your Cash value policy with Term, you can expect the following to take place: Your Term agent will have to prepare a document answering some specific questions about your cancellation, a copy of which will be sent to your current insurance company. If they feel that your Term agent has crossed any lines or misrepresented them in any way, they will report him/her to the commissioner of insurance, who will then be in contact with you. So, if you hear nothing, you're on the right path.

Your present insurer will obviously not like the fact that their cash cow of commissions (you) has turned off the cash tap and will likely call you and try to convince you that your Term agent has misled and lied to you. The most common tactic is to overwhelm you with spurious information, combined with scare tactics, because this mix is proven to confuse and paralyze the consumer. Usually the customer throws up their hands and asks them to stop if they agree to continue with the policy. The best defense: don't take the call.

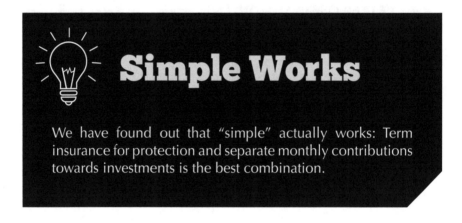

Simple Works

We have found out that "simple" actually works: Term insurance for protection and separate monthly contributions towards investments is the best combination.

Here's a Reality Check on some common Insurance questions:

Question 1: Isn't it smarter to have a permanent life insurance policy so that whenever I die I can leave money to my spouse and kids?

There are a couple of challenges with this idea. First, the death benefit amounts in permanent policies tend to be lower, and the premiums higher than what you would get with a lower priced Term policy. Secondly, you would be paying a large monthly premium for the "investment" part of the policy. If you take the difference in what you're paying between a Cash value (permanent life) policy and a Term policy, and invest that money in any low fee investment vehicle such as Mutual Funds, stocks, or ETFs, you should end up with a larger nest-egg that you can use for your retirement and have money left over for your spouse or children.

Question 2: I don't like paying taxes, so a tax-efficient Cash value policy appeals to me.

Insurance policies are not registered like a 401(k) or a Roth IRA; or, in Canada, like an RRSP, a TFSA, RDSP or a RESP. So if a salesperson tells you that you can take money out of your plan "tax-free," be very suspicious. What the insurance company is actually doing is taking some of the money you paid them and giving it back to you. Sometimes known as a "return of premium," it seems like you're getting a dividend, capital gain, or interest, but you don't have to pay taxes on it. Sounds great, but all the insurance company is doing is giving you back your own money. Of course you're not paying any taxes; the money was never invested in anything.

Question 3: I want to make more money and pay less tax like the richest 1%.

First of all, the mega rich aren't paying less tax than you do because they're investing in Cash Value insurance policies. No, they're involved in complicated corporate structures involving local and foreign corporations and opaque family trusts. The costs of these devices are substantial – probably $100,000+ per year in fees to maintain. You have much more profitable ways to occupy your time and money. If you want to get rich, you need to budget, avoid rip-offs, maintain an active investment portfolio, and be involved in as many successful entrepreneurial opportunities as you can. These will provide for passive income with a minimum of taxes, a lot of learning and, potentially, a lot of fun.

And the Hits Just Keep On Coming....

Were you shocked when you read Mary's story (pg. 59) in which her insurance company kept taking out premium payments after she had cancelled her policy - until they had drained all the cash value in her account? Unfortunately, that's just the tip of the iceberg.

On April 17th 2016, multiple Emmy and Peabody Award winning TV show **60 Minutes** featured a segment called "Insurance industry under investigation" which exposed the systemic practice by the nation's biggest insurance companies of not paying death benefits on millions of policies - even when the companies knew the policyholder had died!

Florida Insurance Commissioner Kevin McCarty said that many insurance companies used the Social Security Administration's Death Master File to their advantage by cutting off annuity, or retirement benefits, to policyholders when they died - but did not use it to notify beneficiaries that they were owed a death benefit. What's even worse, said McCarty, is a practice he discovered involving Whole Life policies in which many insurance companies continued to make premium payments to themselves using their deceased customers' money. **Unbelievable!**

DID YOU KNOW

The average income of the top 1% of earners in the U.S. was $1.24 million, in 2013. An average of $334,800 in taxes was paid on this amount. Yes, they could afford to pay more in taxes, but before we vilify this group, we might want to look at how much we ourselves pay in tax compared to them. Of course when you look at the top 400 earners, who took home an average $265 million in 2013, you might have a stronger case for higher taxes, but our advice is not to get jealous; get busy and get your share.

Key # 6 Make Your Money Work For You.

"
The rich continue to get rich the same way they always have - by understanding how money works and making their money work for them.

Robert Kiyosaki
"

Debt Elimination

Did you just save yourself hundreds or maybe even thousands of dollars by switching to Term insurance from Whole or Universal life? Good for you. You could celebrate your good fortune by taking a fun trip to the islands, or you could turn that extra money into your own fortune. You've already budgeted for that extra expense, so keep using it; just use it more productively.

⚠ Those That Don't Understand Interest Pay It

Your first priority is to get rid of all your high-rate debt. Credit cards are enemy number one here. Have a look at what's in your wallet. Most bank-aligned cards (e.g., Visa and MasterCard) are charging around 19%. Cards from big box stores are charging around 29%. This is at a time when money in your bank savings account is earning you less than 1%, and your average investment portfolio is returning 7%. It's completely out of proportion.

In a perfect world, you wouldn't owe anybody any money. But, there are certain things, such as a house or a car, that are tough to pay for all at once. Happily, these tend to have the lowest carrying costs. We see offers of 1%, 2%, or even 0% financing for new cars. That's a good deal. A 4% mortgage on your house or condo is another example of a good deal. You still want to use every tool available to you (making bi-weekly payments, topping up, or accelerating your payments) so that you get rid of that debt sooner - you really don't want to be paying a mortgage when you retire - but a mortgage isn't your biggest problem. Credit cards are. And, by the way, don't even think of going to a payday loan or check cashing service. They take fees and interest charges to a whole new level. It may sound like a joke, but even the Mob doesn't have the nerve to charge the rates that they do. Avoid, avoid, avoid!

Have a look at this comparison of credit card charges, and then use the Worksheet below it to calculate what you're paying.

Credit Card Comparison Chart

Here's an example of what happens at one national brand retailer if you pay only the minimum necessary every month for $1,000. computer.

Schedule of Payments for One-Time Purchase of $1,000 item no additional purchases; monthly payments $50; interest rate 29.5%.

Month	Balance Owed	Monthly Purchases	Monthly Payment	Interest and Fees	Cumulative Interest and Fees
1	1,000	0	50	24	24
2	974	0	50	24	48
3	948	0	50	23	72
↓	↓	↓	↓	↓	↓
28	56	0	50	1	408
29	8	0	9	0	409

Now let's look at buying the same computer on a low-interest card and see what happens.

Schedule of Payments for One-Time Purchase of $1,000 item with no additional purchases; monthly payments $50; interest rate 6%.

Month	Balance Owed	Monthly Purchases	Monthly Payment	Interest and Fees	Cumulative Interest and Fees
1	1,000	0	50	5	5
2	955	0	50	4	9
3	909	0	50	4	14
↓	↓	↓	↓	↓	↓
21	58	0	50	0	58
22	8	0	8	0	58

Shaving off 7 months of payments and $351 seems like a better deal to us.

The following worksheet will help to determine which of your debts need to be paid off first.

Debt Buster Worksheet

Type of Debt	Interest Rate Charged	Pay Out Balance	Monthly Payment
Credit Card # 1			
Credit Card # 2			
Credit Card # 3			
Credit Card # 4			
Credit Card # 5			
Personal Loan # 1			
Personal Loan # 2			
Personal Loan # 3			
Other			
Other			
Totals			

Investments

As you can see, there are plenty of companies out there making obscene profits on the backs of hard working people. So, how do you get a piece of the action for yourself? It's called investing and it taps into compound interest. It's a beautiful thing. Einstein referred to compound interest as "The greatest invention of the 20th Century."

DID YOU KNOW

Here's a simple example. If you put $2,000 into a savings plan for your new baby and then just forgot about it, when that child turns 60 they would have $608,983 in their account. If, let's say, at age 25 the child then started to add $100/month to that plan, they would have $1,305,948 when they turned 60. There would be taxes to pay, and we're assuming an average of 10% return. Some years will be less, some years will be more, but that's the power of compounding.

The most common financial worry among consumers over 25 years old is being able to afford a comfortable retirement.

2015 LIMRA Study

The Rule of 72

The rule of 72 is a mathematical formula that states that your money will double at a point determined by dividing 72 by the rate of interest. The following chart illustrates this phenomenon, starting with an investment of $2,000 at age 19. Notice how long it takes the investment to double at the three different interest rates.

Doubling time on a $2000 investment compounded at 2%, 6% or 12%.

AGE	2.00%	6.00%	12.00%
19	$2,000	$2,000	$2,000
25			$4,000
31		$4,000	$8,000
37			$16,000
43		$8,000	$32,000
49			$64,000
55	$4,000	$16,000	$128,000
61			$256,000
67		$32,000	**$512,000**

Pay Less Tax, Get Rich Quicker

There are financial vehicles that encourage you to save for your retirement. They are known variously as Individual Retirement Accounts (IRAs.) 401K's or, in Canada, Registered Retirement Savings Plans (RRSPs). They amount to the same thing: encouraging you to save for your retirement will take the pressure off future governments, so they allow you to make money in a savings plan without having to pay any taxes on the gains – for a while.

When you open an account and make a contribution, depending on local laws, that amount may be deducted from your taxes. Inside the plan, you invest in any of the traditional options: stocks, mutual funds, ETFs and so on, but *unlike* benefits from investments made outside a plan, any profits, dividends, or gains you make are not subject to taxation. Over the years of contributing – the longer the better –you gain from compounding without losing any part of it to taxes. When you retire, you should have a substantial nest-egg to draw on. In some, but not all, jurisdictions, when you start to take money out of the plan it will be treated as income, but you will normally pay tax at a lower tax rate because you are retired and not earning as much as when you were employed. The following chart demonstrates how you can pay less tax and get rich quicker.

Comparison of IRA vs. non-tax-sheltered investments.

COMPARISON of an IRA vs. a NON-TAX-SHELTERED SAVINGS INVESTMENT		
Each person deposits $4,000 per year at an interest rate of 12%. Both are in the 40% tax bracket.		
	Person A	**Person B**
	Not Tax Sheltered	**IRA/RRSP**
Value at year 10	$67,824	$74,678
Value at year 20	$195,744	$306,616
Value at year 30	$452,123	$1,026,981
Value at year 40	$965,966	$3,264,324
Note: Hypothetical Example, actual results may vary.		

Credit Rating

When you apply for credit, a lender will look at your credit rating, or score, to determine whether to approve you, how much is safe to lend you, and what interest rate to charge. If the lender sees you as a "high risk" you'll pay a higher rate. If you are seen as a "low risk" you'll pay a lower rate.

The factors that affect credit ratings are:

1. Bank Accounts: By opening both a checking and savings account and managing them well you begin to establish stability.

2. Payments: Whether you pay your bills on time is one of the most telling features of your credit history. Late payments will lower your credit rating.

3. Amount of Debt: How much you owe is a factor in determining your credit score. When using your credit cards, make it a habit to pay off your balance every month.

4. Amount of Credit: Having too much credit may impact your credit rating. Too many credit inquiries may lower your credit score, and having too much credit may make lenders uneasy since there is always the risk you may max out your credit.

5. Major Adverse Financial Events: Bankruptcies, foreclosures and any unpaid child support will affect your credit score.

6. Employment: Being employed means you are able to pay your bills, and your employment status also affects your credit score.

For more information or to check your own credit score, go to one of the following sites:

www.equifax.com

www.experian.com

www.transunion.com

⚠ Cost of Procrastination

By investing $25.00 per week at 9% from age 20 until age 65, you would have $746,041.51. Furthermore:

- If you were to start saving that $25.00 at age 15 instead of 20, you would save $1,175,622.01.

- Thus the cost of waiting until age 20 to start saving would be $429,580.49!!!

Saving Vehicles

Savings and Checking Accounts

A savings account is a step up from keeping your money in a cookie jar because it is safer. Through the Federal Deposit Insurance Corporation (FDIC), or the Canadian Deposit Insurance Corporation, a deposit of up to $100,000 is guaranteed by the respective governments. Caution: Make sure that your financial institution is covered by the FDIC or CDC. The savings account typically pays a very small amount of interest. The benefit here is that your money is available at almost any time you need it. A checking account allows you to easily distribute your money to other people by writing checks and e-transfers, and direct pre-authorized withdrawals with the added security of not walking around with cash. Typically you will pay fees for each transaction, and the interest rate will be very small.

Certificates of Deposit (CDs)

This is a fully guaranteed method of saving that pays slightly higher interest rates than savings or checking accounts. It is locked in for an agreed period ranging from 30 days up to five years, which means that you make more profit, but there are restrictions on taking out your money prior to the end of the agreed term.

T-Bills

Treasury Bills (T-Bills) are government IOUs issued for a term of one year or less. You do not receive interest; rather they are purchased at a discount. For example, you might buy a $10,000, one-year T-Bill for $9,800. The minimum amount you can purchase is $10,000, with increases of $1,000 thereafter. Again, you make a bit more money, but you can't get at it if you need it until the agreed time is up.

Government Bonds

You are lending money to the government, which it will pay back at a predetermined time and rate of return. Some governments offer a tax incentive tied to the issuance of bonds.

Getting Rich

Stocks

With stocks, or equities, you are purchasing shares of ownership in a corporation. You share in both its profits and losses (remember Blackberry or Enron?). You can make money from stocks either by selling them at a profit or by receiving regular income from them in the form of dividends.

Mutual Funds

Mutual funds allow you to pool your money with many others to invest in a broad range of securities. They are managed by experts who carefully monitor the performance of the investments in their specific portfolios, allowing you to sleep at night while they track the markets. In theory these "experts" will do a better job than most in picking the better- performing securities; however, they do make mistakes. Some smart investors pay less attention to the make-up of the portfolio and more to following successful managers from fund to fund. Most mutual fund companies advertise themselves as "no load," which means you pay no upfront fee to purchase them. Back-loaded means that you pay a fee when you sell the fund unless you keep your money in the fund for seven years. That does not mean these are the only fees you pay. Remember, there is no such thing as a free lunch. All funds have a Management Expense Ratio, or MER. This is the amount the company charges for administering its funds. These fees come off the top and typically hover in the area of 2%. So, if your fund says it returned 6% this year, it actually made closer to 8% before management took its fees. Even if your fund returned only 1%, or if **it lost money**, the company still took its fee. Whoever sold you the fund also got paid out of this expense charge. There are some funds that charge very low fees, from 1% to 1.50 %, and can afford to do so because they avoid expensive advertising campaigns. These are, by definition, harder to find, and they may deal only with portfolios of $25,000 and above. For most people who do not want to become financial experts, investing in a Blue Chip or Balanced mutual fund would be a fairly safe bet.

Index Funds

A sure way to avoid making fund companies and their sales staffs rich is to invest in index funds. With an index fund, you purchase small pieces of a large number of companies. The S&P 500, for example, is a grouping of 500 large companies' stocks, which account for something like 80% of all stocks traded in America. The index measures their collective performance. Another popular index is the Dow Jones, which measures the stocks of a narrower group of 30 active, large companies. So, if you invest in the Dow Jones' Index, you're buying a piece of those 30 companies.

The management team of an index fund is a computer, which costs much less to maintain than a group of Harvard business graduates. The upside of an index fund is the low fee, and returns which, on average (though not always), outperform the highly paid experts. The downside is that there is nobody watching on your behalf for a "meltdown" or market correction. Index funds are not great performers in "bear markets," those cautious, slow markets that occur most typically when the economy is in recession, or close to it. An actively managed mutual fund will certainly cost more, but it **MAY** be better equipped to see a meltdown or correction coming enough in advance to rebalance the fund to protect your money; or it **MAY** react more quickly once any market troubles begin. Lots of fund managers do neither. If you are in for the long haul, putting part, not all, of your portfolio in an index fund is a great, low-cost bet. These are easy to purchase through inexpensive online trading platforms such as TDAmeritrade, ETrade, OptionsHouse and Questrade. Remember: if your investments decline, like the January 2015 drop, it's only a "paper loss" unless you sell or cash out.

Dollar Cost Averaging

Most first-time investors simply don't know when is the best time to enter the market and start investing. In the dollar cost averaging method, you put the same amount of money into an investment each month. As the price of the investment rises and declines, you end up purchasing more shares when prices are low and fewer shares when prices are high. Instead of worrying about timing the market (buying low, selling high), you achieve a reasonable average cost per share. You also benefit from compounding because you're not waiting to invest by "timing the market". With the power of compounding and time on your side, you can greatly benefit from this method.

Invest in Your Personal Development

Looking for a guaranteed no-lose investment? Invest in your own personal and professional education. Take some training and development that will help you in your current job, or that will prepare you to start your own business. Simply watching some Ted Talks can be really interesting and might start you down a path that's personally rewarding. Or you can follow thought leaders online, or join associations of similarly minded folks. Another very smart idea is to connect with a mentor. We have loads of other suggestions in our other books, *The ABCs of Making Money* and *The ABCs of Making Money for Teens*.

Key # 7: Start Your Own Business

> ## The biggest risk is not taking any risks.
>
> Mark Zuckerberg

Everywhere you look in the business world there are examples of successful business people who have endured many setbacks before they enjoyed success. Walt Disney was fired from a newspaper because he "lacked imagination and had no good ideas," and his first animation company went bankrupt. Henry Ford's first two car companies failed and left him penniless, but it was "third time's a charm" when he founded the Ford Motor Company, which led him to become one of the richest men in the world. J.K. Rowling was a single mother surviving week to week on welfare payments when she wrote the first *Harry Potter* book. And, let's not forget that Steve Jobs was fired from Apple before mounting a hugely successful comeback and making it the world's biggest company by share valuation. Beyond the satisfaction of building a successful business, there are a number of advantages of entrepreneurship including tax reduction strategies, freedom to call your own shots, creation of a plan "B" to make yourself less vulnerable to job loss, and if the business is successful, virtually unlimited profit potential.

Getting Paid to Play

Sandy has been a passionate crafts person for many years. One of Sandy's favourite pastimes is quilting blankets and other household pieces. Quilting is a labor of love that requires both patience and skill. Over time Sandy learned the various techniques of precision cutting, piecing and sewing. In fact she even tried "top quilting" by hand, which is the decorative patterned stitching that binds the entire project together. She found that she didn't like the finished look of her quilts whether she did it by hand or by free motion on her sewing machine. Sandy was getting very frustrated that her works of art weren't coming together as nicely as she visualized. So she decided to join the local quilting guild not only to enjoy the company of like-minded women, but to see if anyone could suggest a solution.

Soon after joining the guild she heard about a woman who was in ill health and wanted to sell her like-new "Long Arm" quilting machine. It occurred to Sandy that the machine might solve her top quilting challenge and could also turn into a small business by offering this service to other quilters that share the same frustration. The cost for the same machine new was more than $30,000 plus many thousands more for accessories and quilting pattern software. Sandy was able to buy everything for $20,000. The machine, although quite big, easily fit in her basement craft room. She took some introductory courses on how to use the machine and quickly became comfortable teaching herself by experimenting. She now absolutely loves using the machine, and takes great pride in finishing off projects for fellow quilters who are also thrilled with the end result.

Not only is she having a lot fun, but the business is profitable as well. A typical quilt takes around 30 minutes in machine preparation. After that, the Long-Arm does the rest. She charges between $200 - $300 per quilt, and has costs totalling approximately $25 (thread, electricity, batting and an allocation for machine maintenance) per quilt. On a part-time basis, she averages 20+ quilts per month and generates $50,000 in annual income.

If Sandy's story inspires you, it might be the perfect time to assess your entrepreneurial traits. Please proceed to the tool below.

Entrepreneurial Self-Assessment Tool

As you go through the following 15 statements, rate yourself on a score of 1 to 5, 1 being totally not like you, and 5 being totally like you. When answering the questions, be brutally honest with yourself. There is no point in hiding your weaknesses. It's better to identify your weaknesses and plan on how you will compensate for them now rather than later, when it may be too costly.

Entrepreneurial Self-Assessment Tool.

Winning Traits	Entrepreneurial Statements	Self Rating	Area to Improve
Enthusiastic Seller.	I have the ability to influence people towards my way of thinking if I strongly believe in something.		
Networker.	I enjoy meeting new people under a variety of circumstances.		
Tenacious Visionary.	I have a burning passion and work daily towards achieving my goals/objectives/vision.		
Referrer of Great Ideas.	I like passing on great ideas, concepts, messages, or tips to people I like, care about and respect.		
Engaging Communicator.	I have meaningful conversations with many types of people in a variety of circumstances, and I understand the other person's perspective while being able to share mine.		
Proactive Thinker.	I see the opportunities/solutions where others just see the problem.		
Relationship Builder.	I enjoy initiating, building, and maintaining long-term relationships.		
Ethical Decision Maker.	I make decisions and act accordingly based upon my ethics and core values, not simply on profit potential.		
Negotiator.	I have a proven track record of getting what I want and still maintaining a positive relationship as a result of my negotiations.		

Winning Traits	Entrepreneurial Statements	Self Rating	Area to Improve
Evaluator of Risk/ Reward.	I calculate the risk/rewards prior to making any major investment of time, energy, or money.		
Urgency-Oriented.	I believe that time is precious and I don't procrastinate on moving forward on all of my personal and professional priorities.		
Recruiter of Talent.	I am excited about my business/future business and I am looking forward to recruiting great teammates to grow the company.		
Inspirational Leader.	I am known as someone who has the ability to inspire others to follow me towards our common goal.		
Action Driver.	I am a self-starter who is seen by others as an action driver who sets the pace for the entire team.		
Leverager of Resources.	I believe in the power of leveraging time, money, and information and I am always seeking better ways to do things.		

As you can see from Table 5, the first letter of each winning trait spells out the word ENTREPRENEURIAL. Use this as a simple method of remembering what the key winning traits are that you need to focus on to succeed in business. Go back to the tool and review the rating for each of the 15 entrepreneurial statements. Now you will be able to identify and list your strengths (rating of 4 or 5) and your weaknesses (rating of 1 or 2).

Identifying areas of strength. Once you know your areas of strength, you can use those strengths to your advantage as you launch your business. For example, an effective **networker** can take a random meeting with someone, and by tapping into their own **communication skills**, they can learn about that person. As a good sales person they will uncover buying motivators; as a good **negotiator**, they will make sure that they get what they require out of the deal; and as a good **recruiter**, they will attract and **lead** other people to do the same. This example touches on six traits in the Entrepreneurial Self-Assessment Tool.

Identifying areas needing improvement. Now that you have identified your weaknesses, look at ways in which you can address them. Evaluate those areas that require improvement, and consider whether it is possible, and feasible for you to develop the skill, knowledge or attribute to grow in that area over time. If it is feasible for you to develop in that area, then put a plan in place to make it happen.

If you feel that there are some areas that are not as feasible to develop, then consider what you can do to compensate for it – either by working with others (as a business partner, an employee or freelancer) who excels in that area, or by putting processes in place to manage your weakness.

Remember, you don't have to have all the entrepreneurial traits to be successful. If you have the determination to succeed, the rest of the qualities can be learned or acquired. You should also remember that, at least initially, you will be required to be your business' bookkeeper, order department, sales and marketing person, administrator, and at the end of the day, you get to take out the garbage, too. It can be a lot of work but, if you're passionate about what you're creating, it won't seem like work and will actually be a lot of fun. This is why we emphasize that the more you follow your passions; the more successful you're likely to be.

If You Fail To Plan You Are Planning To Fail

If you are committed to setting up a new business, you need some form of a plan. Traditional business plans are very cumbersome and difficult to complete for the average person. So, we have developed the simplest of business plans. If you photocopy and fill in the following charts, and invest the necessary time to obtain accurate information, your chances of success will dramatically increase. As you go through this process you will likely uncover potential challenges that need to be addressed before launching your business. The point of the exercise is to eliminate as many surprises as possible and stack the odds in your favor. This plan, albeit simple, is still a very powerful method of communicating the viability of the business idea to a potential partner, investor or lender.

This chart will help you organize your thoughts in a brief written overview of your business idea.

Getting Rich Business Plan - Business Idea Overview

What does this business entail?
What is the business structure (Sole proprietorship, partnership, limited company?
Who are the business owners?
What products or services will be offered?
What experience, skills/knowledge does the business owner team have in this industry?
Who are the prospective clients?
What is the current need for this product or service?
What is the projected future demand?
Who is your competition?
What are your competitive strengths over your competition?
What are the risks? How will you overcome them?
How much of the startup capital are the owners committing to?
What collateral is available to secure the business debt?
What is the investor's expected Return on Investment?

Projected Sales for Month of:	
Service or Product:	**Amount**
Service 1	
Service 2	
Service 3	
Product 1	
Product 2	
Product 3	
Total Projected Sales for month:	

Projected Upfront Costs:	Amount
Business idea research costs	
Cost to develop a prototype	
Business registration/Cost of incorporation	
Permits/Licenses	
Patent/Copyright registration	
Skills/Knowledge upgrading	
Professional memberships	
Insurance	
Marketing Materials: • Business cards • Letterhead • Brochures • Flyers • Videos • Website • Signage • Paid Advertising • Other	
Business Supplies	
Raw goods and materials	
Purchase/rent: equipment/ tools/ machines	
Professional Fees: • Bookkeeper/Accountant • Lawyer • Consultant	
Total Projected Up-Front Costs	

Projected Monthly Costs:	Amount
Rentals: Office/Storage/Warehouse/Retail Shop/ Furniture	
Vehicles	
Utilities: electricity/water/natural gas/oil	
Parking	
Janitorial/Cleaning fees	
Financial Charges (Banking & Credit card merchant fees, Interest expenses and Bad Debts)	
Refunds or Returned product	
Telephone - Land lines, Internet & mobile phones	
Advertising	
Cost to purchase or produce goods for (re)sale	
Travel, including accommodations & meals	
Postage/courier	
Sales commissions	
Employee wages & benefits	
Insurance	
Taxes: property, municipal, state/provincial	
Total Projected Monthly Costs	

Financial Viability Assessment	
Category	**Amount**
Available Start-up capital	
Total projected upfront costs	
Total projected monthly costs x 12	
Total forecast sales for first year	
Net projected surplus or shortfall	

Now that you have completed The Getting Rich Business Plan and have confirmed the viability of the idea, you can now proceed on your own, or you can approach an investor or lender for financing.

Summary

A final piece of advice is about taking control of your financial situation. When you separate the things that you can control versus the things you can't, you quickly begin the journey to Getting Rich. The following summarizes things that can't vs. can be controlled.

You Can't Control	You Can Control
The economy	Your personal economy
Sustainability of Social Security	Investing for your retirement
Taxes	Taking advantage of tax reductions
Future layoffs	Starting your own business
Rising costs of interest	Eliminating debt
Fluctuations in stocks markets	Dollar Cost Averaging
Rampant Consumerism	Living within your means

By now it should be abundantly clear that anyone who has read and is prepared to apply all of the seven key strategies of this book can get rich. In other words if you commit to doing the following:

1. Have the right attitudes

2. Live within your means

3. Understand insurance

4. Know how much income protection you need

5. Avoid insurance rip-offs

6. Invest wisely

7. Own a successful business, then you will be on the fast track to Getting Rich and living the life of your dreams!

If you found this book helpful and inspiring, you or someone you care about could benefit from either of The ABC Guys' Internationally Best-Selling books.

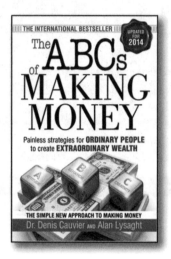 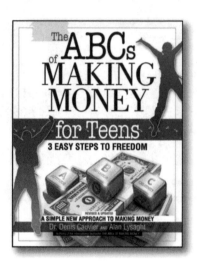

To order these books visit
www.abcguys.com

"America's youth will benefit greatly from learning the basics of starting and owning their own business outlined in this great book."

Fred DeLuca, President and Co-Founder Subway Restaurants

"The ABC Guys have provided a tremendous service in writing this inspirational, common- sense book. They illustrate simple, yet powerful methods of achieving success in finances and life."

Paul Orfalea, Kinko's Founder & Author of "Copy This"